S0-CFK-378

This edition published by Concordia Publishing House
3558 South Jefferson Avenue • St. Louis, MO 63118-3968
www.cph.org • 1-800-325-3040
ISBN 978-0-7586-1662-3

Printed and bound in Singapore

THIS BOOK BELONGS TO

_____

A GIFT
ON THE OCCASION OF

_____

_____

WITH LOVE FROM

_____

DATE

_____

A Child's Book of
PRAYERS

Compiled by
Sally Ann Wright and Susan K. Leigh

Illustrated by
Honor Ayres

CONCORDIA PUBLISHING HOUSE • SAINT LOUIS

Foreword

This book combines prayers of praise and thanksgiving, prayers for ourselves and for others, prayers that have been prayed by generations of believers and those written new for this collection.

The prayers are arranged by theme. Some can be used by adults praying *for* their children, some can be shared *with* children, and some can be used by older children themselves as they bring their concerns to God.

The first section encourages new parents to ask God's guidance and mercy for themselves as they share the joys and responsibilities of parenthood, and to pray for the babies in their care. The remaining sections help children to share their lives with God and to develop a caring heart as they think about others and their needs.

Use this book as a reminder and guide as you, in all times and all places, focus on God, the Creator and sustainer of us all, and to work with Him in partnership as we pray.

Contents

The gift of a child 10

Prayers of thanksgiving 18

Family and friends 28

Everyday living 34

Prayers at mealtime 46

The world around us 50

Prayers for others 56

Prayers for special occasions 64

Prayers at bedtime 78

Blessings 86

The gift of a child

God our Creator,
   thank You for the wonder of new life
   and for the gift of human love.
Thank You that we are known to You by name
   and loved by You from all eternity.
Help us as we learn the joys and challenges
   of parenthood, to live one day at a time
   and to trust You to provide for us as each
   new need arises.

Adapted from the Anglican Service of Thanksgiving for the Birth of a Child

Lord, You are the author and giver of all good things.
Thank You for this precious gift,
  a child to love and nurture, to care for
  and to protect.
We pray for Your love to live in us
  so we may be able to guide with wisdom, discipline
  with love, and teach by example.
May we be encouraging and affirming
  so this child may grow up to love Your Word
  and to walk in Your ways. In Jesus' name. Amen.

Sally Ann Wright

11

Heavenly Father, we thank You
for the gift of this child, entrusted to our care.
May we be patient and understanding,
ready to guide and to forgive, so that through
our love he/she may come to know Your love.
Surround him/her with Your blessing
that he/she may be protected from evil,
and know Your goodness all his/her days.
In Jesus' name. Amen.

The Anglican Service of Thanksgiving for the Birth of a Child

Lord God, we give You praise
  and thanksgiving for all Your gifts.
We thank You that You created us,
  gave us the breath of life,
  and the ability to love others as You love us.
Thank You that You have enabled us to share
  the joys of Your creation in the gift of this
  child.
By Your Holy Spirit, help this little one to grow
  in faith and service to You through Jesus
  Christ, our Lord. Amen.

Adapted from a contemporary service based on the Lutheran Tradition

Bless us, dear Lord, and give us grace
    to love and care for this child.
Give us wisdom, patience and faith.
Help us to provide for his/her needs
    and, by our loving example, reveal the
    love and truth that are in Jesus Christ.
Amen.

The Anglican Service of Thanksgiving for the Birth of a Child

Heavenly Father, Creator of life, You have revealed Yourself in the miracle of the birth of this child. We praise You and thank You for this gift. And we ask that You bless him/her with Your tender care. Through Jesus Christ, who is the Friend of children and the Savior of all. Amen.

Heavenly Father, watch over and bless
this child.
May he/she learn to love all that is true,
grow in wisdom and strength and, in due
time, come through faith and Baptism to
the fullness of Your grace. Amen.

The Anglican Service of Thanksgiving for the Birth of a Child

Almighty God, Lord of the universe, all love,
strength and understanding come from You.
Bless us now with all we need to nurture
the precious gift of this child
and bring us joy in this
new creation. Amen.

Adapted from an Australian Prayer Book

Dear Jesus,
You gave me a new baby,
All little, noisy, warm.
Be with my little baby,
And keep us both from harm.

I know You love this baby.
I know You love me too.
Help me live as a child of Yours
In all I say and do. Amen.

God's Children Pray

Prayers of thanksgiving

For this new morning and its light,
For rest and shelter of the night,
For health and food, for love
    and friends,
For every gift Your goodness sends,
We thank You, gracious Lord. Amen.

Traditional

We thank You, Lord God, heavenly
Father, for all Your benefits, through
Jesus Christ, our Lord, who lives
and reigns with You and the Holy
Spirit forever and ever. Amen.

Luther's Small Catechism with Explanation

Thank You, heavenly Father, for all Your blessings.
For life and health, for work and rest,
For food and drink, for family and friends,
For freedom to choose to love You and serve You,
With all my heart. In Jesus' name. Amen.

Rhona Davies

Thank You, Lord Jesus, for my home and family,
  for food to eat and a warm bed to sleep in
  at night.
Please look after children who have none of
  these things and keep them safe tonight. Amen.

Sally Ann Wright

We give Thee but Thine own,
Whate're the gift may be;
All that we have is Thine alone,
A trust, O Lord, from Thee.

William W. How

Praise God, from whom all blessings flow;
Praise Him, all creatures here below;
Praise Him above, you heavenly host;
Praise Father, Son, and Holy Ghost.

Bishop Thomas Ken

Thank You, God,
  For making the world and all that is in it.
Thank You, God,
  For making my wonderful body and mind.
Thank You, God,
  For my home, my parents, and all the
  people who love and care for me.
Thank You, God,
  For food to eat and clothes to wear.
Thank You, God,
  For leading me to know Jesus, my Savior
  and Lord.
Thank You, God,
  For Baptism and the gifts of the Holy
  Spirit.
Thank You, God,
  For everything. Amen.

A Child's Garden of Prayer

Thank You, God, for the world You have made.
For the warmth of the sun,
For the rain which makes things grow,
For the woods and the fields,
For the sea and the sky,
For flowers, trees and animals,
For families, friends and holidays,
For all Your gifts,
Thank You, God, for the Savior You sent,
For the forgiveness He won,
For the promise of salvation.
In Jesus' name. Amen.

Sally Ann Wright

Creator God, thank You for pets,
   for the special friends we love to play with:
   for furry cats and playful dogs,
   for hamsters in wheels,
   and long-eared rabbits.
Help us always to remember
   to look after them well,
   as part of the world You have made. Amen.

Bethan James

Family and friends

Dear God, thank You for giving us people to take care of us. We know that parents who love us are gifts from You. Help everyone in our family to love and forgive one another for Jesus' sake. Amen.

Little Visits: 365 Family Devotions. Volume 1

Bless our home, dear Lord.
Teach us to love one another,
Support and help one another,
And forgive one another,
As You forgive us through
  Your Son, Jesus Christ.
Amen.

Sally Ann Wright

Thank you, dear God, for my mother
who loves me and cares for me.
Thank you, dear God, for my father
who loves me and cares for me.
Help me to be good,
to listen to them and learn from them,
and to love my parents
as much as they love me.
We love because You first loved us,
through Jesus, our Savior. Amen.

Bethan James

Thank You, heavenly Father, for families:
For moms and dads, brothers, sisters,
Cousins, aunts, uncles
and grandparents.
Help us to love and care for
one another
And to be especially kind
to each one, today.

Sally Ann Wright

Dear God, our thanks for everything:
The sun that shines, the birds that sing,
The flowers that bloom, the wind that blows,
For food and drink that help us grow.

We thank You for the food we eat,
For all the vegetables and meat.
We thank You for dessert so yummy;
We eat it 'til it fills our tummies.

We thank You for this family,
Big or small 'though we may be.
Thank You for this meal, we pray;
Please bless us all in every way. Amen.

More Songs of Gladness

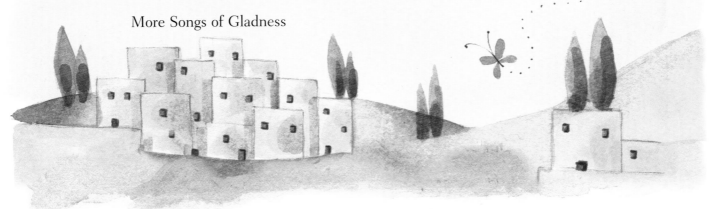

Everyday living

Father God,
   thank You for sleep and bringing
   us safely through another night.
Thank You for a new morning
   and for health and strength.
Lord, be with us throughout this day
   as we eat and work and play.
Fill us with Your love for everything
   and everyone around us. Amen.

Adapted from a morning collect

Jesus, Friend of little children,
  be a Friend to me;
  take my hand, and ever keep me
  close to Thee. Amen.

Walter J. Matham

Heavenly Father, I'm sorry
For the bad things I do.
Forgive my sins and bless me.
In Jesus, make me new. Amen.

A Child's Garden of Prayer

Almighty and everlasting God,
  thank You that You have brought me
  safely to the beginning of another day.
Keep me from sinful thoughts
  and actions, or from running
  into dangerous situations.
Help me in everything I do
  and guide me always to do only what
  is good in Your sight. Amen.

Adapted from a morning collect

Jesus, lead me day by day
Ever in Thine own sweet way;
Teach me to be pure and true;
Show me what I ought to do.
When in danger, make me brave;
Make me know that Thou dost save;
Keep me safe by Thy dear side;
Let me in Thy love abide. Amen.

Little Folded Hands

Christ be with me, Christ within me,
Christ behind me, Christ before me,
Christ beside me, Christ to win me,
Christ to comfort and restore me,
Christ beneath me, Christ above me,
Christ in quiet, Christ in danger,
Christ in hearts of all that love me,
Christ in mouth of friend and stranger.

St Patrick's Breastplate

Lord Jesus,
The wind and the waves obey You.
Deaf people hear because of You.
Blind people see because of You.
Lame people walk because of You.
Dead people live because of You.

Help me to obey You,
To hear You,
To see You in those around me,
To walk where You want me to be,
To live my life serving You in others.

Sally Ann Wright

Lord, make us instruments of Your peace.
Where there is hatred, let us sow love;
Where there is injury, let there be pardon;
Where there is discord, union;
Where there is doubt, faith;
Where there is despair, hope;
Where there is darkness, light;
Where there is sadness, joy;
For Your mercy and for Your truth's sake.

St Francis of Assisi

Lord Jesus Christ, we thank You
For all the benefits You have won for us,
For all the pains and insults You have borne for us.
Most merciful redeemer,
Friend and brother,
May we know You more clearly,
Love You more dearly,
And follow You more nearly,
Day by day. Amen.

Adapted from Richard of Chichester (1253)

Father of lights,
From whom comes every good
  and perfect gift;
Keep us in the light of Christ,
To shine in Your world,
So that all may believe in You.

Based on James 1:17

O Lord our God,
Grant us grace to desire You with our whole heart;
That so desiring, we may seek and find You;
And so finding, may love You;
And so loving, may hate those sins
From which You have delivered us;
Through Jesus Christ our Lord. Amen.

Anselm (1109)

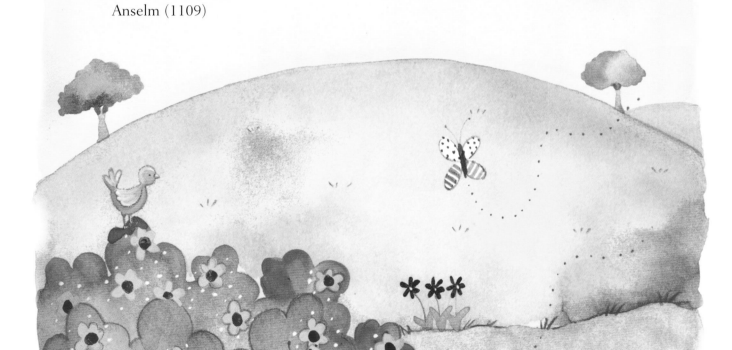

O gracious and holy Father,
Give us wisdom to perceive You,
Diligence to seek You,
Patience to wait for You,
Eyes to behold You,
A heart to meditate upon You,
And a life to proclaim You,
Through the power of the Spirit
Of Jesus Christ our Lord.

Benedict of Nurcia (c. 550)

Prayers at mealtime

Lord God, heavenly Father, bless us
and these Your gifts which we receive
from Your bountiful goodness, through
Jesus Christ, our Lord. Amen.

Luther's Table Prayer

Come, Lord Jesus, be our guest.
And let these gifts from You be blessed.
Amen.

Common Table Prayer

For what we are about to receive,
may the Lord make us truly thankful;
through Jesus Christ our Lord. Amen.

Traditional

We thank You, Lord God, heavenly Father,
for all your benefits, through Jesus Christ,
our Lord, who lives and reigns with You
and the Holy Spirit forever and ever. Amen.

Based on 1 Chronicles 29:11

Be present at our table, Lord;
Be here and everywhere adored.
Thy children bless, and grant that we
May feast in paradise with Thee.
Amen.

Little Folded Hands

Our hands we fold,
    our heads we bow;
for food and drink,
    we thank Thee now.
Amen.

God's Children Pray

For this and all His many mercies,
God's holy name be blessed
and praised; through Christ our Lord.
Amen.

Traditional

The world around us

Our Father who art in heaven,
hallowed be Thy name,
Thy kingdom come,
Thy will be done on earth
  as it is in heaven;
give us this day our daily bread;
and forgive us our trespasses
  as we forgive those
  who trespass against us;
and lead us not into temptation,
but deliver us from evil.
For Thine is the kingdom and the
  power and the glory forever and ever.
Amen.

Thank You for the world so sweet,
Thank You for the food we eat,
Thank You for the birds that sing,
Thank You, God, for everything.
  Amen.

Edith Rutter Leatham

I thank You, my heavenly Father, through Jesus Christ, Your dear Son, that You have kept me this night from all harm and danger; and I pray that You would keep me this day also from sin and every evil, that all my doings and life may please You. For into Your hands I commend myself, my body and soul, and all things. Let Your holy angel be with me, that the evil foe may have no power over me. Amen.

Luther's Morning Prayer

God, be in our heads
And in our understanding.
God, be in our eyes
And in our looking.
God, be in our mouths
And in our speaking.
God, be in our hearts
And in our loving.
God, be in our bodies
And in our doing.
God, be in us; be in us always.
In Jesus' name. Amen.

God's Children Pray

Creator God, You made the world
  And it was very good.
You made light and darkness,
Rivers, streams and mountaintops,
Sun, moon, stars and planets,
Tall trees and tiny flowers,
Silver fish and flying insects,
Birds and beasts, speckled, dappled,
Spotted, striped, and patterned.
Creator God, You made the world
  And it was very good.
Help us to look after it. Amen.

Rhona Davies

God, the Father, bless us;
God, the Son, defend us;
God, the Spirit, keep us
Now and ever more. Amen.

Little Folded Hands

Prayers for others

Lord Jesus, You are the Good Shepherd.
You look after me, and care for me.
Lord Jesus, Good Shepherd,
Look after my family and friends today.

Bethan James

Loving Father,
    please look after all who are not well.
Comfort those who are in pain,
    or who are worried or sad.
Give peace to those who are old
    or frightened.
Help us to be loving and helpful
    to our families, kind to everyone
    we know, and generous to anyone
    who needs our help. Amen.

Rhona Davies

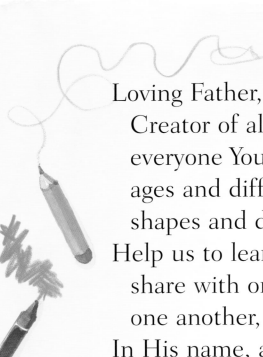

Loving Father,
Creator of all people, You love
everyone You have made: different
ages and different sizes, different
shapes and different colors.
Help us to learn from one another,
share with one another, and love
one another, as Jesus taught us.
In His name, and for His sake. Amen.

Bethan James

For this morning and its light,
For rest and shelter of the night,
For health and food, for love and friends,
For everything Your goodness sends
I thank You, heavenly Father. Amen.

Little Folded Hands

Jesus, help my eyes to see
All the good Thou sendest me.
Jesus, help my ears to hear
Calls for help from far and near.
Jesus, help my feet to go
In the way that Thou wilt show.
Jesus, help my hands to do
All things loving, kind, and true.
Jesus, may I helpful be,
Growing daily more like Thee. Amen.

Little Folded Hands

Heavenly Father, we pray for peace
  in your world.
Where people fight, take away their hate;
Where people hate, fill them with love;
Where people suffer, bring them your peace;
Where people mourn, give them comfort
  and hope.

Sally Ann Wright

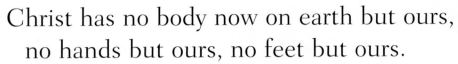

Christ has no body now on earth but ours,
   no hands but ours, no feet but ours.
Ours are the eyes through which must look out
   Christ's compassion on the world.
Ours are the feet with which He is to go about
   doing good.
Ours are the hands with which He is to bless
   all people now.
So Lord, give us able bodies, eyes to see
   the need around us, willing hands and feet,
   to serve You now.

Adapted from the Prayer of St Teresa

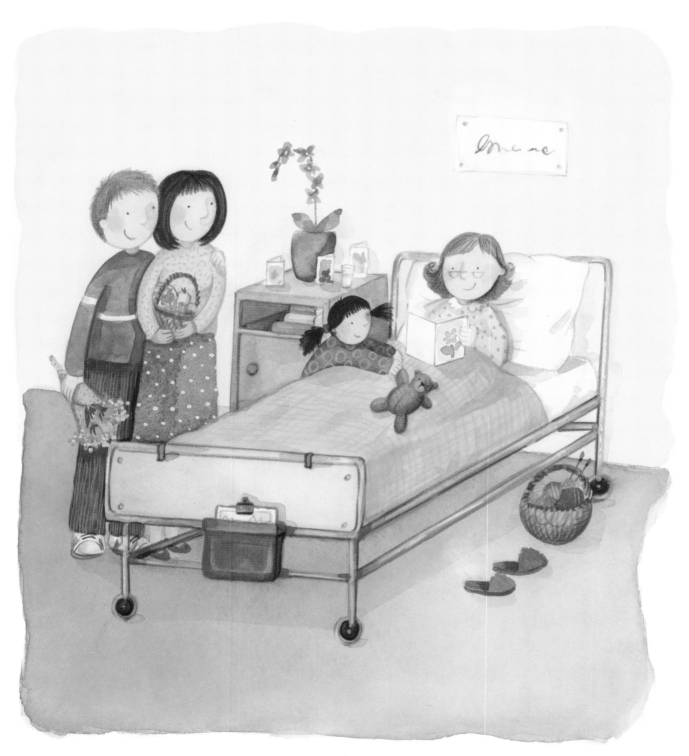

63

Prayers for special occasions

We have a new baby!
   Heavenly Father, the baby is here!
It looks funny; it smells funny,
   and all it does is sleep and eat
   and make lots of noise!
Thank You for this new tiny person
   in our home to love and look after.

Bethan James

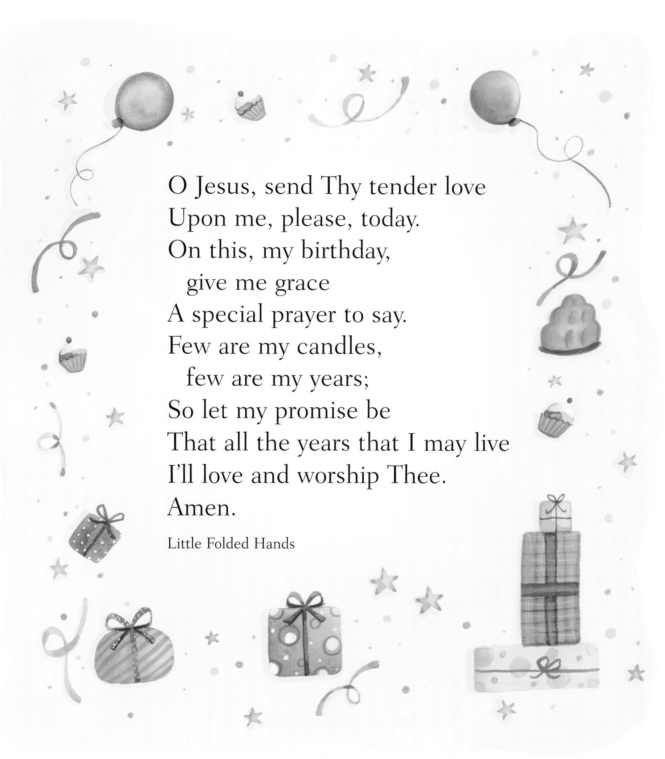

O Jesus, send Thy tender love
Upon me, please, today.
On this, my birthday,
   give me grace
A special prayer to say.
Few are my candles,
   few are my years;
So let my promise be
That all the years that I may live
I'll love and worship Thee.
Amen.

Little Folded Hands

A long time ago, Mary put her baby in a manger.
Thank You, God, that today we can know Him.
A long time ago, the angels sang
   because Jesus was born.
Thank You, God, that today we can worship Him.
A long time ago, shepherds
   hurried to see their Savior.
Thank You, God, that today we can serve Him.
A long time ago, wise men brought Jesus gifts.
Thank You, God, that today we can love Him.

Sally Ann Wright

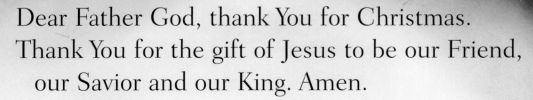

Dear Father God, thank You for Christmas.
Thank You for the gift of Jesus to be our Friend,
   our Savior and our King. Amen.

Bethan James

Lord Jesus,
You were a tiny baby
In a manger, in Bethlehem.
You grew up to be a man
Who healed people who were ill,
Or sad, or lonely,
And you showed us how to love
Other people as God does.
Thank you, Lord Jesus.

Sally Ann Wright

Angels sang, and I will too,
"Glory, glory, Lord, to You!"
Help me sing of Jesus' birth.
Help me work for peace on earth.
In Your name I pray. Amen.

My Christmas Prayer Book

May this new year be a new
beginning for our family.
Dear heavenly Father.
We cannot see what things,
good or bad, lie ahead of us.
Help us to thank You for the good things,
trust You if things are hard for us, and
ask for Your help whatever happens.
At the beginning of this new year, Lord,
hear our prayer.

Rhona Davies

O God our Father,
  please look after our world
  at the beginning of this new year.
Thank You for the message of peace
  that Christmas brings to our world.
Where there is war, let there be peace.
Where there is hate, let there be love.
Where there is sadness, let there be joy.
Where there is suffering,
  let there be hope.
At the beginning of this new year, Lord,
  hear our prayer.

Rhona Davies

Thank You, Lord Jesus,
   that the sadness of Your cruel death
   on Good Friday has a happy ending.
Thank You, Lord Jesus,
   that You died so my sin could be forgiven.
Thank You, Lord Jesus, that You rose
   from the dead so I can one day live with
   You in heaven.
Thank You, Lord Jesus! Amen.

Sally Ann Wright

Dear heavenly Father,
Jesus became a servant to teach us
    how to love, and died on a cross
    that we might live.
Teach me to put other people first
    and to think about their needs
    before my own. For Jesus' sake. Amen.

Rhona Davies

Lord, bless the little children
In all the world, we pray;
Help everyone to love Thee,
And keep them in Thy way. Amen.

Little Folded Hands

God the Father,
    please keep us in Your care;
Lord Jesus, be our constant Friend;
Holy Spirit, guide us in all we do.
Bless us and protect us until we come
    safely to the end of our journey. Amen.

Adapted from a traveler's blessing

Creator God, Lord of all the world,
    thank You for giving us so much to enjoy.
Thank You for new places to see,
    different scenery, different faces,
    different food and different spaces,
    time to spend with people we love,
    and time to meet new people,
    and make new friends.
Creator God, Lord of all the world,
    thank You for giving us so much to enjoy.
In Jesus' name and for His sake. Amen.

Sally Ann Wright

Lord, teach a little child to pray,
And, oh, accept my prayer;
Thou hearest all the words I say,
For Thou art everywhere.

A little sparrow cannot fall
Unnoticed, Lord, by Thee;
And though I am so young and small,
Thou carest still for me.

Teach me to do Thy will today,
And when I sin, forgive;
Grand that, for Jesus' sake, I may
With Thee forever live. Amen.

A Child's Garden of Prayer

May God who clothes the lilies of the field,
and feeds the birds of the sky,
who leads the lambs to pasture and
guides the deer to water, clothe us, feed us,
lead us and guide us, and change us
to be more like our loving Creator.

Based on a blessing from the Anglican Book of Common Worship

Prayers at bedtime

Now I lay me down to sleep;
I pray Thee, Lord, my soul to keep.
If I should die before I wake,
I pray Thee, Lord, my soul to take;
And this I ask for Jesus' sake. Amen.
Little Folded Hands

Before the end of the day,
Creator of the world, we pray
That You, with steadfast love, would keep
Your watch around us while we sleep.
From evil dreams defend our sight;
From fears and terrors of the night. Amen.
Adapted from an evening collect

I thank You, my heavenly Father, through Jesus Christ, Your dear Son, that You have graciously kept me this day; and I pray that You would forgive me all my sins where I have done wrong, and graciously keep me this night. For into Your hands I commend myself, my body and soul, and all things. Let Your holy angel be with me, that the evil foe may have no power over me. Amen.

Luther's evening prayer

Stay with me, Lord God,
  for it is evening,
  and the day is coming to an end.
Stay with me and with all those who
  love You, in the evening of the day,
  in the evening of life,
  in the evening of the world;
  stay with me and with all those
  who love You, now and forever. Amen.

Adapted from an evening collect

Dear Lord,
   look after everyone who is awake
   or weeping this night.
Let angels watch over those who sleep.
Take care of those who are ill,
   give rest to those who are weary,
   help the dying, and give hope
   to the suffering. Amen.

Adapted from St Augustine

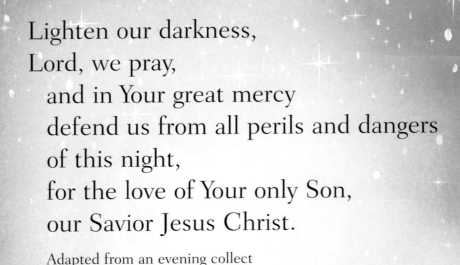

Lighten our darkness,
Lord, we pray,
    and in Your great mercy
    defend us from all perils and dangers
    of this night,
    for the love of Your only Son,
    our Savior Jesus Christ.

Adapted from an evening collect

Dear Father in heaven, look down from above;
Bless daddy and mommy, and all whom I love.
May angels guard over my slumbers, and when
The morning is breaking, awaken me. Amen.

Little Folded Hands

O God our protector, who turns the world
safely into darkness and
returns it again to light: please watch
over us now and keep us safe,
    for You alone are our sure defense

    and You alone can bring us
    lasting peace.
    Amen.

Adapted from an evening collect

84

O God, the source of all good desires,
   and all that is right and fair, give me now
   that peace that only You can give;
   so that I may want to obey Your
   commandments and may pass this night
   in rest and quietness. Amen.

Adapted from an evening collect

May God give us a quiet night,
   and at the last, a perfect end;
   and the blessing of God Almighty,
   Father, Son, and Holy Spirit, be with us
   this night, and for evermore.

Adapted from The Book of Common Prayer

Blessings

Please God,
Bless me when I'm walking,
Bless me when I'm talking,
Bless me when I'm playing,
Bless me when I'm praying,
Bless me when I'm eating,
Bless me when I'm sleeping.
Please bless me every minute
Of the day and night. Amen.

Christine Wright

At the first light of sun:
God bless you.
When the long day is done:
God bless you.
In your smiles and in your tears:
God bless you.
Through each day of your years:
God bless you.

Adapted from an Irish blessing

I'm Your child, for You love me.
You died and rose so I could be
All full of hope and joy and love,
Which come from You, my Lord,
above. Amen.

God's Children Pray

May the peace of God,
   which passes all understanding,
   keep our hearts and minds in the
   knowledge and love of God, and
   of His Son Jesus Christ our Lord;
   and the blessing of God almighty,
   the Father, the Son, and the Holy Spirit,
   be with us and remain with us always.

Traditional

May the Lord bless us and watch over us.
May the Lord make His face shine upon us
   and be gracious to us, may the Lord look
   kindly on us and give us peace;
   and the blessing of God almighty, the Father,
   the Son, and the Holy Spirit, be with us
   and remain with us now and every day.

Based on Numbers 6:24-26

Animals. 26, 27, 51, 77

Arguments 32

Birthdays. 65

Christmas 66, 68, 69

Creation 26, 50, 51, 52, 53

Danger 37, 82

Daytime 18, 34, 35, 37

Disasters. 60

Easter 72, 73

Families 28, 29, 30, 32

Food 18, 21, 46, 47, 48, 49, 51, 76

Harvest 53, 76

Holidays 74, 75

Illness 81

New babies 10, 11, 12, 13, 14, 15, 16, 17, 64

New Year 70, 71

Night-time 78, 79, 80, 81, 82, 83, 85

Peace 61, 71

Pets 27

Suffering 71

Thanks 18, 21, 22, 24, 26, 27, 30, 34, 51,
53, 65, 66, 72, 74, 75, 76

Traditional prayers 39, 41, 42, 44, 45, 46,
47, 48, 55

Unity 58

War 58, 61, 71

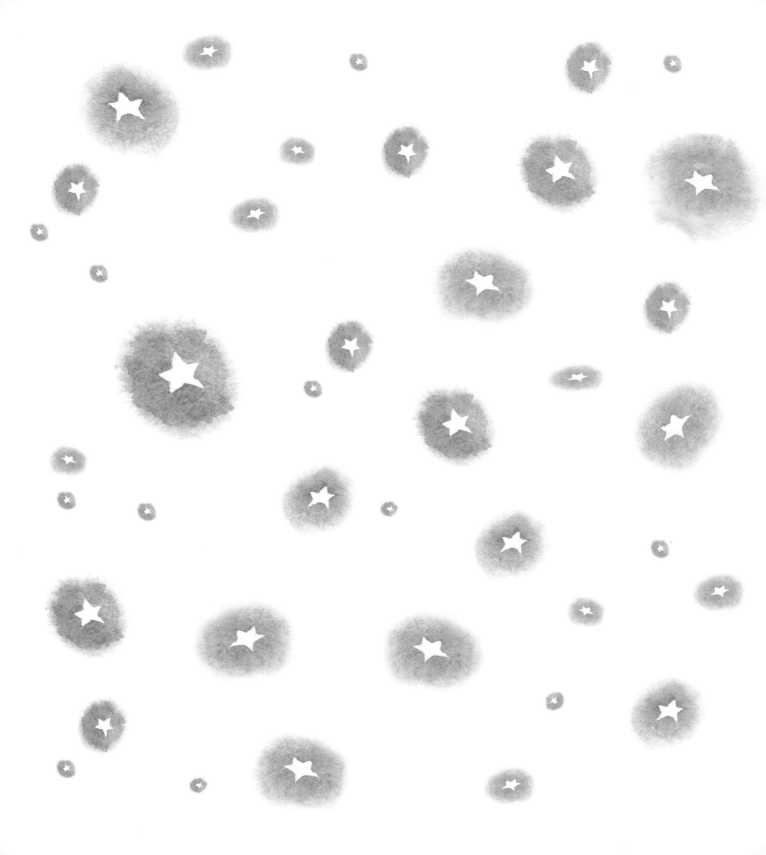